The Story of the
Little Black Dog

by J.B. SPOONER

Illustrations by
TERRE LAMB SEELEY

ARCADE PUBLISHING • NEW YORK

First Edition

"The Black Dog" and "Black Dog (design)" are registered
trademarks of the Black Dog Tavern Company, Inc. Those
marks are used pursuant to a license agreement with The
Black Dog Tavern Company, Inc.

Library of Congress Cataloging-in-Publication Data

Spooner, J. B.
    The story of the little black dog / by J. B. Spooner ;
illustrations by Terre Lamb Seeley.
      p.   cm.
    ISBN 1-55970-239-7
    1. Black Dog (Dog)—Juvenile literature. 2. Douglas, Robert—
Juvenile literature. 3. Dogs—Massachusetts—Martha's Vineyard—
Biography—Juvenile literature. [1. Black Dog (Dog) 2. Douglas,
Robert. 3. Dogs.] I. Seeley, Terre Lamb, ill. II. Title.
SF426.5.S665 1994
636.7'0886—dc20   93-34690

Published in the United States by Arcade Publishing, Inc., New York
Distributed by Little, Brown and Company

10 9 8 7 6 5 4

IMAGO

Printed in China

To Gertrude,
Who loved a good story,
And loved a good dog.

Dedication

T. Lamb. Seeley '98

Of all the boats in Vineyard Haven harbor on the island of Martha's Vineyard, the grandest by far was the topsail schooner *Shenandoah*. She was the queen of the harbor and the love of her captain's life.

Captain Douglas lived alone in a big old house overlooking the harbor. He had lived alone for a long time, and he liked it that way.

One stormy night in early spring, the captain was in his warm kitchen when the back door flew open. In came his friend Eddie, wet and windblown from the northeast gale raging in the harbor.

"Brought you something," he announced even before the captain could close the door.

"She's an orphan," said Eddie, handing him a small black puppy from under his coat. "Found her in a mud puddle. If you can't find a home for her, just take her to the pound. I've got to go. Ferry's leaving for the mainland."

He hurried out the door.

The captain stood there for a moment, jutting out his lower jaw the way he always did when he was thinking. He held the wet little puppy at arm's length up to the kitchen light.

"Now what am I supposed to do with the likes of you?" he said as he looked hard at the shivering pup.

The little black dog squinted at the bright light and yawned.

The captain spread some newspaper down on the floor, wrapped an old blanket around her, and poured some milk into a cereal bowl.

"This berth is *only* for tonight," the captain warned as she lapped up the milk.

The puppy yawned again and went to sleep.

Several days went by. The captain asked everyone who stopped in if they knew of a home for the orphaned pup.

But no one did.

Bernie, who worked for the steamship company that ferried tourists to and from the mainland, came by often. He liked the little black dog.

"Why don't you keep her?" he asked the captain. "You've got plenty of room in this big old house. She'd be good company."

"I don't *need* the company," said the captain. "Besides, Bernie, you know I'm on the *Shenandoah* half the year, and that's no place for a dog. She'd just be in the way."

Then Mrs. Winslow from next door had an idea.

"My daughter in New York City is looking for a dog. Maybe she'll take the pup when she visits this summer. Shall I ask her?"

"Good idea," answered Bernie quickly. "He can keep her till then."

The captain glared at him.

"Ah, she won't be any trouble," insisted Bernie. "How can anything that little be in the way?"

The captain jutted out his lower jaw. "Well," he said finally. "I guess she can stay in the kitchen."

Within weeks the black dog had outgrown the kitchen. Summer was approaching, and the captain left each morning to fit out the *Shenandoah* for the season.

Every evening he came home to find some new mischief.

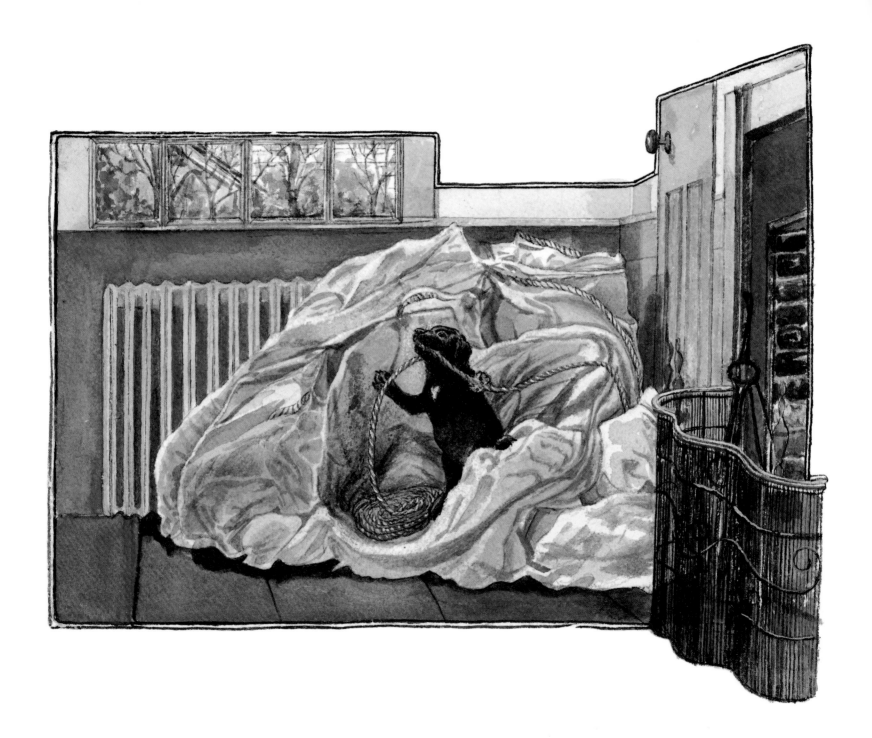

One day the puppy found a huge mountain of cloth tucked away
in a back corner of the house. She was busy pulling and tugging
and ripping and tearing when the captain returned.

"No!" yelled the captain. "Not my *sails! Bad* dog!"

The puppy was so startled, she yelped and ran down the hall
and into the front parlor, where she'd never been before.

It was cold and dark, and the shadows on the wall frightened her even more. As the captain came up behind her, she piddled on the oriental rug.

"No!" he shouted. "Not my rug! Bad, *bad* dog."

Somehow the little black dog just couldn't keep out of trouble. She chewed on the captain's rolled-up charts.

She knocked over his scrimshaw.

She even gnawed on his favorite pair of boots.
"Oh, no! Not my boots!" he roared.

At the end of the day, the captain always found her lying on the sea chest by the window in the upstairs hall, gazing down at the waterfront. "Well," he sighed, "at least you know a good spot when you see it."

The next morning the weather turned warm.

"C'mon," the captain said to the pup. "I have work to do, and I can't leave you here to wreck the place. Let's see if you're any better on board ship."

Down they went to the beach, past the Steamboat Dock, to the Coastwise Wharf. The captain dragged one of the skiffs into the water, and without being told, the little black dog hopped right into the bow.

They rowed out to the *Shenandoah*.

As they came alongside,
the captain lifted the little
black dog through one of the
gun ports and onto the deck.

"Now stay out of trouble,"
he said, climbing over the side.
"And stay out of the way."

The little black dog wagged
her tail.

The captain moved easily about the deck, checking gear and coiling lines.

The little black dog peered through the hatches to the cabins below. The whole world seemed to rise and fall beneath her feet.

"You're just getting your sea legs," the captain reassured her as he disappeared down the companionway.

The little black dog tried to follow him, but the ladder was too steep. She barked, and the captain came back and carried her below.

In the main dining saloon, two long, shiny, gimbaled tables
rocked gently back and forth while the kerosene lamps overhead
moved with the same rhythm.

In the cabins, each bunk
had its own navy wool blanket,
ticking-striped pillow, and
white enameled washbasin.

In the galley was an
enormous iron coal stove
that took up half the room.

Everywhere was the smell of
pine tar, varnish, and damp salt air.

By the time they had to leave, the black dog had found her favorite spots.

While the captain went forward to check the anchor chain, the little black dog jumped, all by herself, through the open gun port into the waiting skiff below.

"Well, what do you know!" he exclaimed. "You're not a *house* dog. You're a *sea* dog!" And for the first time since Eddie brought the wet little bundle into the house, the captain gave the black dog a nice big pat.

Her tail wagged faster and wider than ever.

From then on, the captain and the black dog went out to the *Shenandoah* nearly every day. The crew liked having her on board. She knew where to go when the boat was coming about. She knew which side was to leeward and which was to windward. She knew which portholes had bunks right beneath them so she could get below by herself.

She was never any trouble, and never in the way.

One day, the captain left the black dog at home while he went to a meeting at the town hall. When he got back, he found a note on the kitchen table.

Good news, Captain Douglas!
My daughter from New York was here and just fell in love with your black dog. She had to make the two o'clock ferry, and we couldn't find you, so we took her. I knew you wouldn't mind. If it doesn't work out, she promised to find her another home.
                                                            Marianna Winslow

The captain read the note over and over. He had forgotten all about Mrs. Winslow's daughter. They'd taken the black dog? To New York City?
    He looked at the empty place by the stove and the shred of sail he'd given her to chew on. Then he looked at the clock. It was quarter to two.

Down on the Steamboat Dock, Bernie was surprised to see the
black dog in the backseat of a lady's car.

"Hey, you taking the captain's pup home with you?" he asked
as he reached in the back to pet his friend.

"Yes," replied the woman politely. "She's my new watchdog."

"Well, I didn't think he'd do it, but good luck to you." He sighed
and waved her onto the ferry.

As the last car was being loaded, Bernie glanced down the beach and saw the captain hurrying toward them.

The ferry sounded its horn, and the men on the dock threw off the thick ropes. The captain started waving his arms.

Bernie knew something was wrong. Then he understood.

"Hold it!" he shouted. "Stop the engines!" He disappeared aboard the ferry, shaking his head and muttering.

A few minutes later, Bernie reappeared with the black dog squirming in his arms.

"Guess I got something here that belongs to you," he said, handing the captain the excited pup. "But there's only one problem."

"What's that?" asked the captain, still a little out of breath.

"If you're going to keep her, you have to name her."

The captain jutted out his lower jaw. The black dog licked it.

"That's easy," he said. "I'm going to call her Black Dog. That's what she's used to, and it suits her just fine."